COLOPHON: (kol 'e fon')
1. A publishers distinctive emblem.
2. An inscription at the end of a book, usually with facts relative to its publication.
3. Greek koloph'on: summit, finishing touch, the last word.
   (pronounced "Call-a-fawn" Cafe)

MAMA COLOPHON
(our founder)

Published by
Mama Colophon Inc.
1208 11th St
Bellingham, Washington, 98225
(360) 647-0092

1st Edition 1995, 2nd Edition 1997
Revised Edition 2003
Copyright 1995, Mama Colophon Inc.
All rights reserved.
Printed in the United States of America
These recipes may be reproduced for personal use only.
To order more books, phone
Village Books 1-800-392-BOOK

Fine foods you can make at home!

The Colophon Cafe Best Recipes

Contents (Alphabetical Index on Page 49)

Savory Soups
The Original African Peanut Soup....................3
Split Pea Soup with Garlic Croutons.................5
Cream of Broccoli Soup......................................7
Tomato Parmesan Soup......................................9
Mexican Corn & Bean Sopa.............................11
Thai Ginger Chicken Soup...............................13
Curried Corn & Cheddar Chowder.................15
Manhattan Clam Chowder...............................17
Gazpacho..19
Pollo Tortilla Sopa...20
Salmon Dill Bisque..21

Salad Dressings
Honey Sesame Dressing...................................22
Fat-Free Italian Artichoke Dressing................23
Colophon Caesar Salad....................................25

Spreads
Hummus...27

Best Baked Goodies
Bapple Cookies..29
Peanut Butter Pie...30
Chocolate Cookie Crust...................................31
Pesto Quiche..32
Colophon Pie Crust..33
Broccoli Cheddar or Chicken Pot Pies............34
Parmesan Biscuit Topping...............................35
Peanut Butter Fantasies...................................36
Dave's Breakfast Cookies................................37
Low Fat Muffins..38
Colophon Cookies...39

Our Personal Favorites
Ray's Turkey Chili...41
The Yogi's Banana Bread................................43
Old Marge's Cheesecake.................................45
Chocolate Chunk Cake....................................46
Chocolate Frosting..47

"Ancient drums echoed eerily through the lush green jungle as a scantily clad Tarzan carefully stirred the thick soup in his treehouse kitchen hoping fervently that Jane would swoon over his culinary efforts and melt into his arms in an uncontrollable passion."

*From
" Tarzan and the Magic
Ginger Root"
by Mama Colophon*

MAMA COLOPHON
(our founder)

The *Original* African Peanut Soup

This often-copied-never-duplicated recipe was created in the fall of 1985 from a recipe for African "Ground Nut" Stew, ("Ground Nuts" being Peanuts). The ginger root, chilis and garlic give it a distinctive, spicy taste which some people call "addictive".

The Colophon featured this recipe in the "Coasting & Cooking Cookbook" by Barbara Williams, a book of recipes from the finest restaurants on the Washington coast.

Blend in food processor	1-ounce fresh ginger root, scrubbed & chunked.
	2-cloves garlic
	1-teaspoon crushed chili peppers
Add to processor and chop. (leave chunky) Then add to soup pot	3 1/4 cups canned or fresh diced tomatoes
	1 3/4 cups dry roasted unsalted peanuts.
	1-med onion - chopped
Add to soup pot.	1 1/2 cups chicken stock
	4 cups canned or fresh diced tomatoes
	3-cups water
	1/2 lb cooked and cubed turkey or chicken
Make a paste of	1/4 cup melted butter
	1/4 cup flour

Add as needed to thicken mixture to pot, and heat to 160º

Reduce heat to 145º. Thin with water to desired consistency. (For a vegetarian version, leave out the turkey and use a vegetable based stock instead of chicken stock)

Garnish with peanuts

Serves 6-8

"As the fog crept across the grey winter harbor, Captain Vancouver peered out at the heavily forested coastline, exclaiming, 'Thick as pea soup, this blasted weather,' and went below for a pint."
  from "The History of Fairhaven"
  by Mama Colophon

Split Pea Soup
(Thick as Fog)

*Our simple, healthy version is vegetarian and low-fat.
We garnish it with our own homemade croutons.*

Lightly saute in a little butter — 1 cup finely diced yellow onion

*Bring to a boil.
Cook covered on simmer
for 1 to 1 1/2 hours or
until carrots are done.*

5- cups water
1- lb green split peas (rinsed)
1 med sized diced carrot
salt & pepper to taste

Thin with water

Serves 6-8
Garnish with Colophon Croutons.

Colophon Croutons
Use as a garnish for soups or salads.

Cube enough day old bread to cover a cookie sheet.
Mix together:
1/2 cup melted butter
1 teaspoon each of garlic, thyme, parsley and tarragon

Drizzle butter mixture over bread, stiring cubes around.
Bake at 400 degrees for 8 minutes. Stir well. Put back in oven until toasty brown. Cool before serving.

"It did not matter one iota that the president hated his broccoli, thought the White House chef. It was his duty and right to fix it for him anyway."

*from "Picky Eaters in Politics"
by Mama Colophon*

Cream of Broccoli Soup

A rich and creamy winter's day soup created by the Colophon to make everyone a broccoli fan.

Saute in 1 Tablespoon butter or olive oil until tender	1/2 white onion - chopped 2 cloves garlic - minced 2 stalks celery - sliced thin
Add and bring to boil	1 cup of water 1 tsp. salt (may be omitted) 1/2 teaspoon white pepper squeeze of a lemon dash of Tabasco 2-lb thawed frozen or fresh broccoli (chopped)
In a separate bowl, combine and whip until smooth, add to pot & heat to 160º (Do not boil!)	4 oz softened cream cheese 1 cup warmed milk
Make a paste of and add to soup	2 Tablespoons melted butter 2 Tablespoons flour

Reduce heat to 145º
Thin with milk to desired consistency.

Serves 4-6
Garnish with Grated Cheddar

"Ah, mama's soup, so divinely fragrant as the family gathered on Sunday afternoons around the red wine and crusty bread and shared tales of the business done the week before."

*From " My Bovine Vinnie",
by Mama Colophon*

Tomato Parmesan Soup

Friday is always tomato soup day at the Colophon. This Italian flavor soup is easy to make and excellent any day of the week!.

In a soup pot, saute in 1 Tablespoon butter or olive oil until tender

1/2 med onion - chopped
2 cloves garlic - minced
1/4 cup chopped parsley

Add and heat to 160º

2- 15 oz cans tomato soup
1- 15 oz can diced tomatoes
(or equal amount of fresh)
1/2 teaspoon black pepper
1/4 teaspoon thyme

Serves 4-6
Garnish with shredded parmesan cheese

For a variation if you prefer cheddar cheese, add 1/4 cup of sherry and 1 cup chopped cheddar cheese to the soup mixture and warm to 160º. Garnish with cheddar wedge instead of grated parmesan.

"Zapata leapt swiftly from the moving horse, stormed quickly into the large house, and after having been gone some six long weeks, strode not to kiss his waiting wife, but to the kitchen for a hearty bowl of soup"

*From " The Passions of Zapata"
by Mama Colophon*

Mexican Corn & Bean Sopa

One of the most popular soups ever to come from the Colophon, the Mexican Corn & Bean Sopa has been featured in many publications since we created it. It's vegetarian, low in fat and delicious.

Saute in a little olive oil	1 medium finely diced onion 3 cloves minced garlic
Add to soup pot and heat to a slow boil	1-15 oz can diced tomatoes (or equal amount of chopped fresh tomatoes and tomato juice. 2- 15 oz can red kidney beans (drained) 1- 24 oz can vegetable juice
In a small bowl mix, then add hot water to a paste-like consistency, Add to pot and heat	3 teaspoons chili powder 1 teaspoon sugar 1 teaspoon cumin 1/2 teaspoon black pepper
Add to pot, and heat to 160º Simmer for 1 to 2 hours.	1- lb bag of frozen corn kernels

Thin with water or vegetable juice

Serves 6-8
*Garnish with blue and yellow
Tortilla Chips*

"'This soup is so good that every Tuesday shall be known as Thai Tuesday!,' exclaimed the queen."

*from "The King and Thai"
by Mama Colophon*

Thai Ginger Chicken Soup

This extraordinary, exotic soup won the 1995 Allied Arts Soup Festival in Bellingham.

Cook until rice is done	2 1/2 cups chicken broth 1 cup rice
Add to soup pot, cook until temp. reaches 160º	1 Tablespoon "Taste of Thai" Green Curry Base* 1 Tablespoon garlic powder 2 teaspoons thyme 2 teaspoons basil 1 Tablespoon fresh ground ginger root 1 lb chopped cooked chicken *(Curry base contains: chilis, onion, garlic, galanga, lemon, kaffir, lime peel. We sell it at the Colophon if you can't find it)
Turn heat down slightly and add	1 14 oz can coconut milk Dash of lime juice Dash of lemon juice

Serve at 150º ~~~~ Thin with water if desired
(rice will make mixture very thick)

Serves 4-6

Garnish with fresh parsley

"Certainly it is well known that the cow is a sacred being', Ghandi began slowly, 'but this cheddar soup does inspire one to respect it even more."

from "The Divine Bovine"
by Mama Colophon

Curried Corn & Cheddar Chowder

The second-place winner at the 1986 Chowder Cook Off in Bellingham!

Whip together in soup pot	1 quart hot water 6 oz softened cream cheese
Add and heat to a slow boil	1 16 oz can creamed corn 4 teaspoons curry powder 1 teaspoon black pepper 1/2 cup chopped onion
Add and heat to a slow boil	1 1/2 lbs frozen corn kernals 2 stalks chopped celery
Add, reduce heat to a simmer	Roux (3 Tablespoons flour mixed into 3 Tablespoons melted butter.)
Stir gently into soup	1 cup cubed & floured cheddar cheese (tossed and shaken in a bag with 2 Tablespoons of flour)

Serves 6-8
Garnish with cheddar cheese grated or cut into shapes

"..And while we're at it, we'll take a few clams, too."

from
" The Purchase of Manhattan, 1626"
by Mama Colophon

Manhattan Clam Chowder

*The Colophon used to serve only a white chowder, but we gladly embraced this wonderful red version created by our soup chef.
It's spicy, delicious and simple to make.*

In soup pot add, cover with water, and cook until potatoes are done.
- 1 diced med white onion
- 3 small cubed potatoes
- 1 peeled, diced carrot
- Juice from two 6 1/2 oz cans of chopped clams
- 1 8 oz bottle clam juice
- 2 Tablespoons parsley
- 1 diced red pepper
- 2 Tablespoons instant mashed potatoes
- 1 tsp thyme
- salt & pepper to taste

Add to soup pot, Heat to 160º
- 1- 14 1/2 oz can diced tomatoes juice and all
- 2 cups vegetable juice
- the cans of clams without the juice

Serves 4-6
Garnish with Goldfish Crackers

"'Gazpacho!', he declared as his partner sneezed. His friend remembered after that to hold his breath while opening the black pepper."

from
" Pat & Dave's Excellent Kitchen Adventure",
by Mama Colophon

Gazpacho

A traditional, spicy cold tomato soup. Excellent for a summer meal.

Mix together the day before serving in a large bowl and chill overnight.

3-15 oz cans diced tomatoes or equal amount diced fresh
46 oz vegetable juice cocktail
1/4 cup chopped white onion
3 cucumbers (peeled, seeded, diced)
1/2 bunch celery (diced)
1/4 bunch cilantro (minced)
1 bunch green onions (chopped)
2 Tablespoons olive oil
2 Tablespoons minced garlic
A good dash Tabasco
1 tsp salt
1 tsp black pepper

*Thin with chilled vegetable juice cocktail if too thick.
Chill pot and bowls in freezer before serving.
For added flavor serve with shrimp and a dollop of sour cream on top!*

Serves 6-8
Garnish with Tortilla Chips

New recipe to this cookbook!

Pollo Tortilla Sopa

The idea for this unique soup was borrowed from a street vendor in La Paz, Mexico.

Saute onion and garlic in hot oil until onion is tender. Add chicken, cook about 5 minutes

2 Tablespoons oil
1 medium onion (diced)
5 cloves garlic (minced)
1/2 lb chicken (cooked, cubed)

Blend until liquid in food processor, add to pot.

2 - 1 lb cans tomatoes

Add broth and spices, heat to 160º

6 cups chicken broth
2 teaspoons oregano
1 teaspoon cumin
1 teaspoon marjoram
1 teaspoon thyme
1 teaspoon black pepper
1 teaspoon salt

mozzarella cheese (shredded)
sour cream
avocado
tortilla chips

To serve: Fill soup bowl 1/2 full with broken (not crushed) tortilla chips, cover chips with shredded mozzarella cheese, fill with hot soup.
Garnish with sour cream and/or avocado and whole tortilla chips.

Serves 6-8

New recipe to this cookbook!

Salmon Dill Bisque

By popular demand, a rich and creamy Northwest favorite!

Combine and puree in food processor	1 carrot, medium 1 red pepper, small 1 green pepper, small 1/2 onion, small 1 celery stalk, diced
Add spices, cover with water and cook until done	1 tsp garlic, granulated 1 tsp dill weed 3/4 tsp pepper 2 Tablespoons lemon juice
Whisk in roux to thicken	Roux (mix 3 Tablespoons melted butter with 3 Tablespoons flour)
Turn down slightly and add	8 oz. smoked salmon, deboned and chopped in food processor
Thin as desired	1 pint Half n Half

May be garnished with a dash of dill weed or a fresh sprig of dill

Serves 6-8

Honey Sesame Dressing

A great dressing with an oriental flair.

In food processor or blender combine	1/4 cup chopped onion 1 tsp fresh chopped ginger root
Add	2/3 cup honey (softened in microwave).
Mix in mixer	2 cups safflower oil 1 cup cider vinegar
To Mixer add	1 tsp soy sauce 1/2 tsp salt 1 tsp paprika 1/2 tsp dry mustard powder

Add food processor mixture to oil and vinegar in mixer. Add 1/3 cup toasted sesame seeds. (if you need to toast the seeds, spread on a cookie sheet and bake at $350°$ 20-25 minutes until light brown.) Mix and refrigerate.

Shake well before serving!

Fat-Free Italian Artichoke Dressing

A "good" fat-free dressing is such an unusual thing, that when "Gourmet Magazine" discovered we had one, they wrote and requested our recipe!

Chop in food processor	1 cup artichoke hearts (packed in water, drained)
In Mixer add:	1/4 cup chopped onion 1/2 cup apple cider vinegar 1 cup water 1/2 cup apple juice concentrate 1/4 cup minced garlic 1/8 cup honey 2 tsp basil 2 tsp oregano 1/2 tsp white pepper

Mix in artichoke hearts and refrigerate.

Shake well before serving!

"This is the dressing which I have made!' the emperor declared. 'It shall be known as Caesar's'"

*From
" The Idiots of March",
by Mama Colophon*

Colophon Caesar Dressing

Several Colophon Chefs contributed their best home Caesars to this dressing. We make it without eggs.

In a shaker bottle add   1/2 cup olive oil
5 cloves pressed or minced garlic
1 Tablespoon lemon juice
2 teaspoons Worchestershire Sauce
1 teaspoon Dijon Mustard
freshly ground pepper

Shake to mix and refrigerate.

Toss together in a large bowl with lettuce, grated parmesan cheese and homemade croutons. Serve with french bread.

*For variations on this,
add shrimp, smoked salmon or avocado to the salad!*

Shake well before pouring over salad!

"Hummus? Isn't that something you grow in shady places?"

*from "Vanna Meets Martha Stewart"
by Mama Colophon*

MAMA COLOPHON
(our founder)

Hummus

An exotic blend of healthy stuff that tastes great on bagels, as a vegetable dip, or on vegetarian sandwiches.

Puree in food processor for 3 to 4 minutes.

- 4 cups cooked, drained garbonzo beans
- 2 teaspoons cumin
- 2 teaspoons salt
- 1/2 cup minced garlic
- 1 cup olive oil

Add

- 1 15 oz can or jar of Tahini (ground sesame seeds)
- 1 3/4 cups lemon juice

Blend in food processor until thoroughly mixed, then refrigerate.

Makes approximately 4 cups of Hummus

> *"'Boss, dee plane!' he cried, heading for the landing strip and the shipment of decadent desserts which surely must have arrived."*
>
> *from "Fantasy Food Island"*
> *by Mama Colophon*

Bapple Cookies

Like "trail mix" in a cookie, many people eat just these instead of a full lunch!

Cream together in a large bowl	3/4 cup butter 3/4 cup white sugar 1/2 cup brown sugar 3 eggs-add one at a time
Add	3/4 teaspoons vanilla 1/2 cup apple juice 1/8 cup cooled espresso
Mix together	2 1/2 cups flour 2 teaspoons baking soda 1/2 teaspoon salt 1/2 teaspoon allspice 1/2 teaspoon nutmeg 2 teaspoons cinnamon 3 3/4 cups oats
Stir in and mix well, scraping sides and bottom of bowl	1 med chopped apple 3/4 cup raisins 3/4 cup chocolate chips 1/2 cup chopped walnuts

-Drop rounded spoonfuls of dough onto parchment lined cookie sheet.
-Dip fingers into cold water and press cookies into round, flat patties. (They will not spread.)
-Sprinkle each with 1/2 teaspoon chopped walnuts.
-Bake at 325º 10-12 min or until light to med brown.
Do not overcook.

Makes about 2 dozen large cookies

Colophon Peanut Butter Pie

*This pie is so delicious, "Bon Appetit" requested our recipe and printed it in the August, 1993 issue.
This recipe makes 2 pies.*

Mix together in a large bowl and set aside.	18 oz cream cheese 1 1/2 cups crunchy pnut butter 1 1/2 cups brown sugar 1 teaspoon vanilla
Whip on low speed for two minutes	Two cups heavy whip cream
Add and whip on high speed until peaks form (do NOT overwhip or cream will turn buttery!)	1/2 cup powdered sugar
Fold	The whipped cream mixture into the peanut butter mixture.
	Mixture into two 8 inch Chocolate Cookie Crusts. Spread evenly and freeze pies for 3 hours.

Recipe continued on next page...

Colophon Peanut Butter Pie Continued...

Melt in separate Bowl   2 cups melting choc (or semi-sweet choc chips) with 1/2 cup half & half in the microwave for 30-45 seconds. Stir until smooth

Top Pie   Carefully spoon half the chocolate ganache on the top of each frozen pie. Spread evenly and quickly garnish with 1 Tblsp chopped peanuts before the chocolate sets. Chill for 1 hour before cutting. Use a knife dipped in hot water for cutting.

This recipe makes two pies.
They may be frozen for storage.
To thaw, place in refrigerator for several hours.
They will cut more easily if partially frozen.

Chocolate Cookie Crust

For the Colophon Peanut Butter Pie

Combine well by hand or food processor   4 1/2 Cups finely ground chocolate cookie crumbs
1/2 Cup Butter Melted

Divide in half and press into two pie tins.
Bake 7-10 min at 350º

Pesto Quiche

Traditional egg pie with an Italian touch.

In unbaked 9" pie shell, layer half the mozzarella, the pesto, the sun-dried tomatoes and the remaining cheese.

3/4 cups ready-made pesto
1/2 cup sun-dried tomatoes
2 cups shredded mozzarella
1 pie shell

Blend together

4 eggs
1 1/2 cups milk

-Pour batter over top of tomato/cheese mixture.
-Bake at 400º for 10 minutes, or until crust is lightly browned.
-Reduce temperature to 300º and bake until quiche is set and knife comes out clean.

Quiche may be made out of almost anything!
Simply fill a pie shell with three cups of ingredients-meats, cheeses, or vegetables, and then pour egg mixture over the top. For added flavor on many quiches, add 1/4 tsp dry hot mustard, and 1/4 tsp cayenne pepper or a dash ground black pepper to the egg mixture.

Makes one Quiche

Colophon Pie Crust

For use with recipes for quiche or fruit pies.

Blend in food processor for 10 seconds-no more. Mixture should be a course meal.

1/2 lb unsalted butter, cubed
2 1/2 cups white flour
1 teaspoon salt
2 teaspoons sugar

Add slowly to running food processor. Blend until mixture just holds together. No longer than 30 seconds.

1/4 - 1/2 cup ice water

-Turn dough out onto pastry cloth. Divide in thirds and pat into disks.
-Wrap in parchment and refrigerate for at least one hour. (do not overwork this dough!)
-Flour a pastry cloth and roll dough from the center to the edge, turning pastry cloth and adding flour as necessary.
-When fitting into pie pan, allow about 1 1/2" extra dough.

Makes 3 crusts. *Crusts may be frozen after fitting into pie pan if they are wrapped well.*

Broccoli Cheddar Pot Pie

A rich and flavorful pot pie with a parmesan biscuit topping.

Microwave on high until potatoes are soft; place into large bowl	1/2 cup butter 1 lg onion, chopped 2 carrots, peeled & diced 3 celery stalks, sliced 2 lg potatoes cut in small cubes 1/4 cup sherry 2 Tbls minced garlic
Microwave for 3 minutes, or until it can be blended together. Pour mixture over the vegetables.	3 cups milk 1 cup grated cheddar or processed cheese spread
Add to vegetable mixture and mix thoroughly. Scoop 1 1/2 cups of mixture into oven proof soup bowls. Top with parmesan biscuit rounds (recipe on next page). Brush with egg white.	50 oz canned cream of potato soup 1 cup cheddar cheese shredded 3 cups chopped broccoli (if using frozen, thaw first) 1/4 tsp white pepper 1/3 Tblspn garlic powder

-Bake at 350º for 20-25 minutes until bubbly and golden brown
-**Makes 6 large pot pies**

For a Chicken Pot Pie, use 3 1/2 Cups cooked, diced chicken instead of broccoli, and add 1/8 tsp Sage and 1/4 tsp Rosemary.

Pot Pie Parmesan Biscuit Topping

Mix on slow speed of mixer just until blended

2 cups flour
1 Tablespoon baking powder
1 teaspoon sugar
1/2 teaspoon salt
1/2 teaspoon pepper
1/2 teaspoon paprika
1/2 cup parmesan shredded
2 Tablespoons chopped green onions

Add butter pieces and mix until coarse. Blend in milk.

1/3 cup unsalted butter cut into 1/2 inch pieces
3/4 cup milk

-Turn out onto a floured board and knead until the dough is no longer too sticky to work with.
-Roll out dough to 1/4" thick .
-Cut dough with paring knife, tracing around top of an upside down soup bowl.
-Place biscuit rounds on the filled bowls.
-Brush tops with egg whites .
_Bake at 350º for 20-25 minutes until pot pies are bubbly and golden brown.
Makes 6 large pot pie toppings

Peanut Butter Fantasies

Decandently special dessert bars.

Cream together	3/4 cup butter
	3/4 cup brown sugar
	1 egg
	1/2 teaspoon vanilla
Add and mix	3/4 cup wheat flour
	3/4 cup white flour
	1/2 teaspoon baking powder
	1/4 teaspoon baking soda
	1/4 teaspoon salt
Press Mixture	Dip fingers in water and press mixture into greased and floured 9 X 13 inch pan.
Bake	325º for 15 minutes, or until crust is lightly browned
Cream together and spread over top of crust	1/2 cup butter
	2 cups crunchy peanut butter
	1/2 teaspoon vanilla
	1 cup powdered sugar
Sprinkle on top of peanut butter	1 1/2 cups semi-sweet choc chips

Bake pan in 325º oven for 1-2 minutes to melt choc. Garnish w/toasted coconut. Chill before cutting.

Dave's Breakfast Cookies
Low-Fat cookies make great tasting healthy snacks.

Mix together in mixing bowl	1 1/2 cups applesauce 1 1/8 cups brown sugar 1/2 cup apple juice 1/6 cup orange juice 1/6 cup lemon juice 2 Tablespoons vanilla
Mix in	1 mashed banana
Stir in	3/4 cup flour 1/2 cup wheat flour 1 Tablespoon baking soda 1/2 Tablespoon cinnamon 1/2 Tablespoon nutmeg 1/2 Tablespon ginger 3/4 teaspoon cloves
Stir in	4 cups oats 2 cups rice crispies 3/4 cup crushed cornflakes 3/4 cups dried fruit

These cookies are very moist. It is easiest to use an ice cream scoop and drop the dough on a parchment lined cookie sheet. Dip fingers into water and pat cookies into flat circles. They will not spread while baking.
Bake at 325º for 12-15 minutes.

Makes 24 Cookies

Low Fat Muffins

*Health Clubs buy these from us.
They taste too good to be low fat!*

Mix on high speed for one minute to break up whites	1 cup sugar 5 egg whites
Add and mix	2 teaspoons vanilla 3/4 cup applesauce 1/2 cup nonfat sour cream 1 cup buttermilk
Combine and add to wet mixture. Do not overmix!	3 3/4 cup white flour 1 1/2 Tablespoons baking powder 1 teaspoon baking soda 1/2 teaspoon salt
Stir	1 cup fresh or frozen fruit into flour mixture

-Fill paper muffin cups.
-Sprinkle lightly with sugar.
-Bake at 325º for 15 minutes or until pick comes out clean.

Makes 8 Large Muffins

Colophon Cookies

One of our hottest selling cookies.

Cream	1 cup butter 1 cup brown sugar 1/2 cup white sugar
Add and mix	2 eggs 1/2 Tablespoon vanilla
Add	2 cups white flour 1 teaspoon baking powder 1 teaspoon baking soda 1/2 teaspoon salt
Add	1 3/4 cups oats 1 1/2 cups Rice Krispies 3/4 cup white chocolate chips 3/4 cup butterscotch chips 3/4 cup pecans

Drop batter onto nonstick cookie sheet.
Bake at 350º until golden

Makes 20 medium or 10 giant cookies

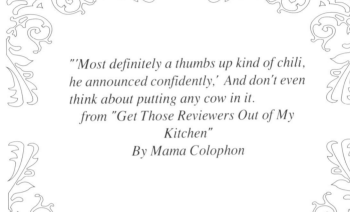

"'Most definitely a thumbs up kind of chili, he announced confidently,' And don't even think about putting any cow in it.
from "Get Those Reviewers Out of My Kitchen"
By Mama Colophon

Ray's Turkey Chili
An amazing chili made without beef or beans!

Heat oil in a large soup pot and add these, stirring until cooked

3 Tablespoons vegetable or olive oil
1 chopped red onion
1 chopped yellow onion
2 chopped leeks
6 chopped garlic cloves

Mix these together, adding just enough of the beer to form a thin paste. Stir paste into cooked vegetables.

2 Tablespoons flour
4-6 Tablespoons chili powder
1 Tablespoon oregano
1 Tablespoon salt
2 Tablespoons cumin powder
1 to 2 teaspoons cayenne pepper
bottle of cold beer

Add and stir well

3 lbs cooked chopped turkey breast
2-14 1/2 oz cans stewed tomatoes (with juice)
1-14 oz can tomato sauce
4-5 Tablespoons of the beer (drink the rest)
1 Tablespoon peanut butter

Stir often and simmer on low heat 2-5 hours. Add beer or water to thin, but not too much.

Serves 8-10
Garnish with chopped onion and cheddar cheese. Serve with tortilla chips or corn bread.

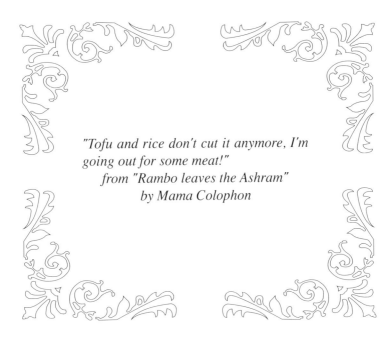

"Tofu and rice don't cut it anymore, I'm going out for some meat!"
   from "Rambo leaves the Ashram"
      by Mama Colophon

The Yogi's Banana Bread

Discovered in the '70's by a Yogi in Bellingham

Mix in food processor	1 cup brown sugar
	1/2 cup softened butter
	2 eggs
	3 or 4 very ripe bananas
Add to food processor and blend thoroughly	2 cups flour
	1 teaspoon baking powder
	1/2 teaspoon salt
	1/2 teaspoon baking soda
	1 teaspoon cinnamon
	1 teaspoon cloves
	1 teaspoon nutmeg
Add to food processor and blend very lightly	1 cup frozen blueberries
	1 cup chopped cashews

Bake in well greased loaf pan at 325º for about 1 hour. Test with a knife to see if it's done in the middle. Remove from pan and set on wire rack to cool.
Slice and serve.

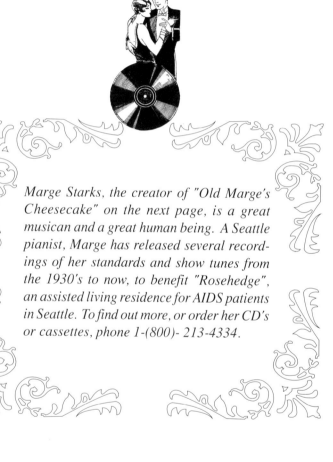

Marge Starks, the creator of "Old Marge's Cheesecake" on the next page, is a great musican and a great human being. A Seattle pianist, Marge has released several recordings of her standards and show tunes from the 1930's to now, to benefit "Rosehedge", an assisted living residence for AIDS patients in Seattle. To find out more, or order her CD's or cassettes, phone 1-(800)- 213-4334.

Old Marge's Cheesecake

Marge's son Jim taught us how to make this divinely rich cheesecake while we were in college. He once sold them to restaurants in Cannon Beach, Oregon.

Mix in food processor and press mixture into bottom of glass pie pan to form a crust *Bake crust 10 minutes at 375º*	1 pkg (1/4 lb) Graham Crackers (crushed) 3/4 melted stick of butter 1/4 cup sugar
In mixer, blend until smooth and pour into crust *Bake again for 20 minutes*	2-8 oz packages softened cream cheese 2 eggs 1/2 cup sugar 1 teaspoon vanilla
Mix by hand	1 cup sour cream 1/2 teaspoon vanilla 1/2 teaspoon lemon juice 2 Tablespoons sugar

Pour mixture over pie and smooth with knife or spatula. Bake again for five minutes.
Remove from oven, cool and refrigerate.
Serve very cold as is, or with berries on top.

Makes one pie

Colophon Chocolate Chunk Cake

One of our most requested decadent dessert recipes, this one keeps them coming back!

Whisk together and set aside	2/3 cup cocoa 1 cup boiling water
Cream together then add the cocoa mixture	3/4 cup butter 1 1/4 cup brown sugar 2/3 cup white sugar 2 eggs 1 egg yolk 1 Tablespoon vanilla
Blend together and mix on high speed for 30 seconds	3 cups white flour 1/2 teaspoon salt 2 teaspoons baking soda
Add slowly mix on medium speed scraping bowl often for 30 seconds	1 2/3 cups buttermilk

Pour batter into greased and floured 10 inch cake pan and bake at 350º until knife inserted comes out clean. Cook thoroughly and frost with Chocolate Frosting.

Makes one layer cake

Colophon Chocolate Frosting

Very rich, creamy frosting for Chocolate Chunk Cake or any other homemade goodies.

Cream together	1 cup soft butter
	1 1/2 cups cocoa powder
Add and mix well	3 1/2 cups powdered sugar
Add very slowly to mixer	1/2 cup half & half

Mix all together on high for 15 seconds, scraping bowl thoroughly.

Frost cake and garnish top with whole milk chocolate chips or grated chocolate.

Frosts one layer cake

The Colophon Cafe Best Recipes

Alphabetical Index

African Peanut Soup, The Original....................3
Banana Bread, The Yogi's 43
Bapple Cookies..29
Breakfast Cookies, Dave's 37
Broccoli Cheddar or Chicken Pot Pies............34
Caesar Salad, Colophon 25
Cheesecake, Old Marge's 45
Chocolate Chunk Cake....................................46
Chocolate Cookie Crust...................................31
Colophon Cookies...39
Chocolate Frosting..47
Cream of Broccoli Soup....................................7
Curried Corn & Cheddar Chowder.................15
Gazpacho...19
Hummus...27
Honey Sesame Dressing..................................22
Italian Artichoke Dressing, Fat-Free 23
Manhattan Clam Chowder...............................17
Mexican Corn & Bean Sopa............................11
Muffins, Low Fat 38
Parmesan Biscuit Topping...............................35
Peanut Butter Fantasies....................................36
Peanut Butter Pie...30
Pesto Quiche...32
Pie Crust, Colophon 33
Pollo Tortilla Sopa 20
Salmon Dill Bisque 21
Split Pea Soup with Garlic Croutons..................5
Thai Ginger Chicken Soup..............................13
Tomato Parmesan Soup..................................... 9
Turkey Chili, Ray's 41

A big thank you to all Colophon staff, past and present, who contributed their culinary knowledge and special recipes to the Colophon Cafe.

MAMA COLOPHON
(our founder)

"Nowhere can I think so happily as in a train...I see a cow, and I wonder what it is like to be a cow, and I wonder whether the cow wonders what it is like to be me."

-A.A. Milne